AF321981

About the Author

Billy MacKinnon is a feature film writer, editor and playwright. He currently lives in Athens and Berlin.

NEXT

BILLY MacKINNON

www.vineleavespress.com

A NOUS AMOURS
you know who you are

BERLIN

Of children
and forests
and a man's voice calling.
Of the interminable stairs
up to my lover's arms,
and the separate colours of our skin,
dark on light, light on dark.
Stone by stone, in
hope of resurrection
and boiled cabbage,
the women rebuilt this place
over the pits and charnels
of their sons and husbands,
of this city redrawn
in the aesthetics
of the drawing board,
and behind the chainstores and perfume stalls
still the seep of massacre and piss
yet well-remembered.
Evil crossed the sea.
He passed it on the way.
His name was Adil.

He stood on this balcony
and smoked
and froze
in the novelty of Autumn,
not home,
shoveling his poverty
in the toil of disbelonging.
Yet he came to love this place
as I did.
We met one morning.
Him, I didn't know,
some kind of job then
I supposed.
I was sleepless and hungover
in the indolence of my profession,
but the morning quickened
in the warmth of casual greeting,
in the continuity of being,
and no unshapely difference
between us
nor nation,
nor enmity
nor silence
nor the deformity
of statehood.

FUCKING ARTISTS

Beer and misery
two birds
flying backwards
the misadventure of grammar
and the desk and its frights
of poetry and its point
and the involuntary word
did it cough?
was there blood?
Can't help it
fucking artists
we do what we do
no sense
a door slams in a wind
of some foreign place
and we set up home
in this house of cards
sure the view was good
it always is
of words untold
words retold
then the nags

and the damn fathers
over your shoulder
but a tune called something
played itself
to the chord of nothing
my face
a question mark
yours
an exclamation mark
and the ink got everywhere,
out of the bottle
onto my cuff,
my hands
the front of your blouse
even the cat and its paws
and over the tablecloth
over the carpet
and down the stairs
and over the lawn
and out
into the night.

ON MY FATHER'S 80ᵀᴴ BIRTHDAY

Four score years in the human boat
no shore as such
no land to speak of
and our voices are so faint
even this fine rain
drowns us out

there is nothing wrong with sadness
or just this sea
where we lost each other
or just this night
life heals itself
the ship of memory
forty fathoms sunk
and the body remembers
in the jetsam of floating things
the miracle of toes
in the ocean of memory

lamb
you called me

wee lamb
as you ridiculed my thinness
and failed to blunt the sharpness
of my tongue

I will buy a smart new suit for your funeral
and maybe
just maybe we could laugh about that

but quick now —
something to cure these trembling hands!

then sinking
we sink in each other.

FACTORY

We were death at the window
our faces
in our tailcoats and Ascot bonnets
this Spring morning
after the night
after the wedding party
the factory farm
the window
peep and keyhole
onto another s' nakedness
and no more polite way to say it:
pigs
pork factory
two hundred eyes and snouts in there
(more, probably, impossible to count)
warehoused in concrete
under permanent neon
crush naked pink and panic
at the very sight of us
stampede
flesh piled on flesh
from one unyielding corner to the next

and wealth and death
as ever
seated side by side in there
and fear crouched by
all looking down and on

We were death at the window
nobody laughed
only breakfast lay ahead of us
over the fresh grass
in the company of flowers and shoes
and chablis glasses
and Milli took an old invite slip
from a sling bag she'd borrowed from a friend
and fixed it above the window
in broad sunlight
and wrote on the back of it
in lipstick:
Do
Not
Disturb
The
Workers.
And that was it
and over the lawn
and into the waiting cars.

TOURIST

You bargained like an Arab
so you thought :
end of business
day without profit
was our only weakness
that,
tourist
and your wallet
our silence.

day's end
we gathered up our goods
into our blankets
and quit the pavement
and shouldered our burdens
as best we could
and home
to an uncertain evening
of a day without light
and you
the hotel steps
into the sanctuary of white tablecloths
and serving staff and cut flowers.

as it is said
our weakness
your advantage
and will always be so
as your wisdom would have it
as we are told
and seen to be
a thing of curiosity
among the monuments and ruins
all things beyond repair

But even so
a word, then
tourist
on our behalf
from night and sleep and its doorways
for the abandoned
for the idlers
the widows and thieves
and liars and water carriers
for the driven mad
whose shadows
cross the *maidān* at midnight:
it may always be thus
the ragged balance sheet
the night shifts
and quiet hallways and numbered doors
our womenfolk
to kneel and dust
the street from your shoes

perhaps it all comes to the same
and yet a word
a word of caution
just for the record
for the disgrace of it
to each thing
its price
and so
a word of warning
tourist :
tourist
count your change.

Marrakesh/Athens

TO THE SEA

No up ahead
no vanishing point
only the vanishing.
Night has left her luggage
on the upstairs landing
night has
moved in for good:
the relic ancestors
in their gilded frames
have lost
their powers of
recollection
consult the
book of shades
as though the shadows
had it:
hallways
cabinets
window seats
carpet slippers
the dark of night
the dark beneath the earth

what difference?
the candle snuffs itself
an eye
the nursery keyhole
nursery sunlit within
consults the
book of shouts and screams
as though the daylight
had it:
there are no signposts here
nor roads
no timetable of trains
nor track to lead us out
only the cemetery gates at midnight
the firelight on our hands
only the pointing finger
points and speaks :
to the sea
to the sea.

LOST BUTTON

I have mislaid my overcoat
some place by the river
I think
I will wait here this night
out in the grass,
as the sky turns on my face,
and the seven stars,
the seven sisters,
hang on their exquisite threads,
and the moon beams fully down on me :
the moon - the mother
of all buttons.

I will dream
the comfort of wardrobes,
of tribes and teamwork,
of chatter, conflict, controversies,
brothers in buttonhood
and sisters,
each in its fashion,
a parliament of buttons,
deep into the night.

We imagine things.
This sky,
this firmament : pole star, dog star,
creatures cruel, fantastic,
sketched in needlepoint,
I offer up
my candidate,
this coronation,
newcomer
to the ranks of the divine menagerie,
this ascension -
the Celestial Overcoat.

My friend will come,
will find me with his two eyes,
mine, mine are four,
the better to see the true dimension of things,
how little provenance there is in this world,
how few things endure
in the scale of ownership and loss
I have lost my overcoat.
The grass will cradle me.
The mother of all buttons shines on my face
and I will dream of questions,
like
to whom to do I belong,
to what,
and so will pass the night.

HILDE

Face it
Hilde
you're dead.

You were such a liar all your life
we both knew that
I almost loved you for it
the sheer tireless scale of it
but tell me now
is there a hell for liars?
or how I see it
history's worst 100
all in a tiny
hellish lock-up
each lying to the other
for all eternity
each retelling
infinitely larger than the last
so even the Devil
will come and eavesdrop
from time to time
looking for ideas.

You write from hell again
Hilde
write of that
or better still
lie of it
As I remember you
your feet up on the arm of the couch
gazing at your shoes and
the wallpaper beyond
bored
and in a mood for trouble
you say
why not ask them over
you have something important to tell them
and to bring a bottle
you will put a genie in it
and who knows?
maybe a little cash
will do nicely
too.
Still
this place still has its ways
to pass the time
rumours
gossip
raincoats
that kind of thing
still ways to pass the evening
and so a note
so news for you
from this solid world

of daylight and lamplights
what's in
what's out
what was
or never will be
you were such a liar all your life
so this
my love's token to you
this my sentiment
my latest offering to you

Lies
Hilde
by return post.

NEXT.

the debt matures
the world turns
in its sleep
and forth
and back
and back again
and forth again
the flying thread
the shuttle
on its magic loom
the ins and outs
of things
what's in
what's out
what's new
what's up
what's next
next is an appetite
next
is a finger
pointing the way
five
is a fist

two is fuck you
finger your neighbour
finger your lover
stuck in the dyke
of things to come
join the procession
wipe your bum
next
a page is turned
a story told
and then? and then?
follow the plot is
next
is next in line
footsteps following
one foot
after another
keep in step
keep in time
next
the list
of lists of things to do
timetables
cancelations
fate and its inspectors
on every platform
selfsame word
same destination
same sign
on every face
same question mark
the waiting room

a sleeping car
the wheel marks out
the metal track
in measured doses
an accident up ahead
one thing
leading to another
next thing you know is
what comes next
next love affair
next morning after
next memory
the dining car is
next is an appetite
time is an appetite
forget to steel yourself
this is your final waitress
coming
worlds fly past
world turns in its sleep
and stepping downwards
through the vaulted earth
falters
fades
forgets
and we
are stopped
and
still.
Next.

(For the physical poets. Seoul performance international korea.)

5 Histories

FAIRY TALE

Of this
I will not speak lightly
nor of what crime
I say I am blameless
I slept
in open sunlight
in the song and heat
of the cicadas
a stone for a pillow
and woke
in the shade of a tree
its shadow leaning over me
who would have thought
a tree
could have such violence in it?
fooling itself
I suppose
it was some vengeful god
in some form or another
its shadow's weight
leant heavy on my thighs and shoulders
and put its rape on me
and I carried its child.

The birth was complicated
a hen's brown egg
large for its type
out of the passage
of one ear
yet I swaddled it in the warmth
of my apron pocket
and went about
my daily tasks.

A season passed
I woke
by candlelight
the eggshell cracked and empty
on my bedside table
as on the far wall
next to the oak and laurel jars
swelled in infancy
a bee
my child
of quite unnatural size
I pressed you close
into my breast
and you betrayed me
my son
and stung me
and the curse of prophecy
entered my blood.

Seasons passed
how many changes
can a mind endure?
how much foresight?
or put more plainly
I woke
with the head of an ox
on my shoulders
or so I imagined
or so they told me.

Down at the quayside
I drew the crowds
I healed a leper
and a cripple
cast off his crutches
into the sea
and swam out
to his death
and a childless woman
whom I advised
to abandon her husband
or all
at least
in so many words

Then the sailors
I did not care to cure them
of the comfort
of their drunken nights and days
such is the way of wanderers and outlaws

abducted me
and tied me in their ship's hold
drifted port to island port
fed me obscenities
and would have a ring
put in my nose
like a dancing bear
for the profit of it
yet I forgave them
their simple cruelties
and prophesised
instead
their imminent deaths.

And so a mountaintop
which did not interest me at all
a shrine they called it
more a pit
of skulls and thigh bones
and I the Queen
in her robes and ashes
while my attendants
the charlatans
pocketed the funds

They came afar
Athens
and Corinth
peered down on me
wildly focused in their terror
and their questions

to one man I answered
(for he was obviously dying)
'go down to market' I said
'and the first words you hear,
that is your oracle'.

I do not mean
to speak in riddles
it's just how words come out
these days
or how I hear them
and how they
come to me

ignore me
do
nor ask me my advice
why would you?
over the endless traffic
noise pursuing noise
ignore this nuisance
hovering your café tables
and a coin in her paper cup
my words reduced to nonsense
mere ramblings
for ancient ears alone
cannot be heard
in this age of plainspokeness
or ask
and I might not answer you
nor put the fear in you

of my apparent madness
if I could speak now plainly,
plainly,
if I only could.

FABLE

Half-boy, half man
creature
fabled composite
a skinny boy in shorts
climbs the hill up to Lykavitos.

A laughing man
exits a yellow cab.

A girl in sunglasses
down the hill
washed-out tee shirt
cut-off blue-jeans
in fact
quite shabby
this girl
but on her feet
golden sandals.

Across the way
young woman
dressed entirely in black

clutches infant
to her breast
which is in fact
a loaf of bread.

Now this man
seated on a milk crate
under the shade of the supermarket awning
what heresy committed
what divine misjudgement?
turned into this
was once a bird perhaps
or tree
or wandering stone
wandering the broken pavements
or dog most certainly
to sleep in your darkened doorways
while under the street between themselves
the mice
are whispering prophesies of him
this dog turned man:
turned man
to wear
this worst
this cruelest injustice :
the leash
and collar
of humanity.

PALACE

Comings goings
defeat everywhere
such are the benefits
of silence and its policies
such rumours
of the known world.

The tethered rope
the driven stake
of radius and diameter
such is the stuff of mind
and its perimeters:
to gaze out further
the wilderness beyond
is simply tiresome:
evening comes
the beast
the goat turns
circles homewards
returns
its captive post
its exile home.

You are already known to me
a face foreseen
a boy
with a boy's ambition
you will greet me
on the palace steps
will embrace me
like the lost returning father
and I will hold you to me
smiling in return
a history foretold
my child
my innocent
my assassin.

And all of you
there will always be
you
the cleaning ladies
always the suds
the rag and basin
to erase the deed
the disgraced and dead
to lift
and carry away
and kneel and scrub
hands chaffed and raw from
so much use
and talk among yourselves
and cautiously agree

in whispered undertones
this place
so long as time and power
endures
this palace
this tiled floor
has seen blood again enough
for one day.

ISLAND

Nor let our bitter looks deceive you
Stranger
these are just the faces life has given us :
we will wear them

and tell of how
it came to pass
over the salt waters
out of that grave
we call the sea
from out the East
abandoned
it was said
an infant's coracle
and winter's gale and night
her sole attendants
and rush and fern
and swaddling thorn
her only coverlet
and stormbird
the name we gave her
for the sea that brought her

or St.Briony's wort
that she might bear at least
some mask of sanctity
for we feared this girl child
who yet grew in time
into a kind of womanhood
and rose in years
and journeyed out
and found
and plucked
so it was said
the very rod
from out her father's womb
and thrust it
staff and wand
into the sod
where root and leaf
it grew
and she came again among us
and made us silent
that she might speak clearly
how this seed
would bare that fruit
that beast might eat
but man
and man alone
should be born to know and understand
and she would have us
taste of it

And so we barred our doors
against her
and nail and hammer
hanged the little man
of cob and sheaf
our evenings sanctuary and comfort
over the lintel stone
the knotted string
to tie and untie
that the storm might carry her away
that she might wander
staff and rags
and take her counsel elsewhere
among the beasts of moor and cloud
her natural brood and congregation

There is a track
as it is said
above a well
over the far side
to where the way leads down
the running deer
the trail
at sunrise
into the forbidden shade
the sweet grass there
a place where the stream
springs from its source
a secret place of trespass
place of listening
place of madness
and so became her place of augury

and gnawing solitude
and set up her abode there

We care nothing for such things here
but the shuttered night
a table set for daybreak
of our menfolk
man and child
in simple sleep its peace
this shared bed and blanket
how we will lean into them
and stop their ears
if needs be
how it will fall our due
the womenfolk
the listening ours
to hear alone
this night in wakefulness
of how her fate has come to this
the end of all unwanted things
of the famished heart
the screech owl
the cry and banished rage of it
of flight
over our hearths and rooftops
the blown wind
the sky
her solitary car and transport
between one silence and another
of the spin and weave
of sour prophecy and lies

a death foretold
the sailor drowned
the infant dead to crib
of son and father slain
all of it
and the rest
we will have none of it

Of needless things
there is
nothing more to know
nor need be known
nor certainty
nor wisdom
save the furrowed field
and yoke
of the uncertain plough
uncertain future
nor messages
nor messenger
of heavens plots
and purposes
and other suchlike rumours
we will set our hearts against them
that we might serve
the common bond
of earth and man
make sure the waking day
the evening's homeward tread
lay clear the earthen track
of mortal innocence

which is their birthright
to this effect
there is no other world
nor ever can be
that they might bless
the common shore
of tides and hours
of common findings
common home
and set aside complexity
of man and its divisions
and so will multiply
so endure.

PLACE

Why did you leave your home
you say
and take the road
no windows lit
only the moon
a sullen bitch
dogging at your heels
and you will say
how far
before this night ends?

Answer me
old night
then here is my reply
of one foot following the next
we will sleep by your roadsides
you and I
we will sleep in your ditches
we will turn together
turn in our sleep
this turning world
and up ahead a dark

and mighty chorus
the sea
a million voices
million drowned
all of one voice
to usher us in
one single voice
to beckon us
one single throat
to swallow and consume.

So do not talk of me
I have not heard of whom you speak
listen
she is at my back again
sniffing me out
her moonlight
only the questioner's searchlight in my eyes
put it away
I have no secrets left for you to feed upon
nor light nor dark to blind me
who am blind enough.

Who knows this place
this time
of once upon a time?
no time to speak of
nor voice of it
nor day to shine
nor night to fall
nothing at all

nothing at all
no single thing
to put a name to
nor this
nor that
nor even nothing
nothing at all
who knows this place?

There is a story going round
should the want arise
a sailors' song perhaps
of the far and near of things
the common tides
to spirit them away
the constant stars
to trick them home again
for it is written
a workmens' song perhaps
the flawless heavens'
shoddy handicrafts
of plasterboard
and plaster ceilings
how we fell
so it is said
the fall
being long and hard
onto this granite floor
of broken legs
and heads :
sing it elsewhere

the strength and silence
of hidden things
are all that counts
it is the beggar's cup
of nothing to declare
it is the barefaced lie
the pointless contraband
the knife in your shoe
a checkpoint up ahead.

Once
it was enough
out of the cradling womb
a red-balled fist
out of the ninth month's
bedmate's mouth
unliving word
whose rhyme is breath
and stars took flight
over the roofs and fields
helmeted
in horns
like demon princes
in their drunken carts
the driven mad
a paradise
gone off its head
so knock and enter
be let in
it is only the halfway-house
of back
to where you came from.

Watch me
I will plead my innocence
in the skin of a goat
and on that sea of lies
a sinless boat
the tide was up
we charted course
and gagged the little ones
so we might pass beneath
in silence
nor rouse the dogs
out of their basket dreams
of dance partners and dinner bowls
the way was hard and long
there is an end
even to unwanted beginnings
the unspoiled shore
our steps made landfall
this place
this time
of once upon a time
of solid ground
the magic fact
the conjured trick
who knows this place?

A Season of Pomegranates
(Athens, 9 days, 9 notes)

1. SEASON

The season of pomegranates
gives way to the season of oranges
Autumn comes gently here
as off the back
of a fruit seller's cart.

2. MUSE

I know
I may not look so normal
and glad of that
and happily admit
I make mistakes
wrong table
nearest the public bench
I do not notice them to begin with
seated in the shade
of the *periptero*
they notice me alright
a kindly interest
in this
their natural victim
but nothing doing
I have nothing left to offer
to each only a cigarette
or maybe a light
they are elderly enough
these women
quite elderly
but on their feet

from time to time
out on this street of tourists
hawking their shawls and bedspreads
which no-one wants
I look away in shame
and down at the white tablecloth
and up again
seven now in all
around this bench
heads grey
in black attire
black widows
seven muses
they see me
each of them
the muses
of dejection
of defiance
muse of poverty
muse of pride
of song
from another world
of labour without profit,
muse
of lifetime's face
cracked in withering sunlight
of pavements
of unspoken thoughts
muse
of forebearance.
I leave my table

my back to them
they call out to me
I turn
half-fearing a curse
the very oldest
blows a kiss.

3. BABYSITTER

The babysitter
three small black children
white nanny
the Nanny's Tale
her dress this morning
deep carmine
the plastic grocery bags
skinny legs and arms
open to sunlight
dress drawn at the waist
brood trawling on behind
and their shouts and complaints
I'll tell your story
If I dare.

4. GIBBET

An old double mattress passes on the pavement
(far side, four legs
four hands
a beast
of sorts
a holy relic)
on its way to the rubbish dump
what do these stains speak of?
a menstruation
a vomit
after a hard night's ouzo
a wet dream
nosebleed
heavy fever
coffee spilled
by lovers
by a lonely man
love
spilled
red wine
a murder
miscarriage

birth
death
passes on the street
speech from the gibbet
on its way to the garbage heap
to the pyre
speech of the condemned man
foul-mouthed
to the last
a history
spoken in its own words.

5. STEP

She sees him
runs to him
throws off her hat
her sudden hair tumbled over her shoulders
he takes a step backwards
now
her
a few paces behind him
their faces grim and unsmiling
silence between them
have they quarreled ?
obviously
the curious thing :
they are walking perfectly in step.

6. SILENT

A silence
at these hours
falls over this city
an antique silence
one imagines
commands attention
commands our silence
though in itself
stands speechless
silent in its nakedness
silent in its nudity
is a dripping tap
a solitary girl
and her bouzouki
quiet
on the marble emptiness
of a cafeneion floor
is a naked boy
cold as stone
turns in his sleep, stirs, reawakens
to the sound of his own voice
ornamental

washed-up
on some municipal rooftop
flows as a dream flows
out of the city
down to the harbor
past the ferry boats
and hawkers and ships' mates
past the information booths
and evening timetables
quits the port
out to a sea of
comings goings
voices destinations
as the far horizon
keeps its distance
and hints of infinity
but does not give the game away
so holds its tongue
so keeps its peace
and is silent.

7. ULYSSES

She's seen it
the lot
as much as can be seen
through one pair of eyes
don't be fooled by appearances
her tired look
her chair on the street
her chain smoking
hardly a stranger passes
but greets her
the aimless young
the homebound secretaries
the bead and pencil sellers
with their black faces
the waiters between their shifts
or the elderly
raking the public garbage
by dead of night
dead of night
for the shame of it
Don't sing to me
of ageless Aphrodite

Antigones
Erigones
Penelopes
of bold Ulysses...
or his dog.
You have to sing at all
you lot
if you insist
sing of her.

8. BALCONY

She takes the teacup
and leans and drops it
over the parapet
'Bone china' they said,
rather precious.
that's how long it takes:
merely a second.
She gazes over, down at the pavement
the pavement gazes back,
a hard look in its eyes,
daring her,
a dare.
The cup
no longer that
a shattered thing
a thing for the street cleaners
not that they come anymore
not since the war began.
And who would anyway remember its story
this cup?
of cradling hands and intimate small talk
through the winter evenings

of warmth
and fragile sweetness
and the touch of lips
the scented rim
the scent of something
both failed to put a name to
then deep into the night
the hidden comforts
of a kitchen shelf
and stacked
and safe
wiped clean
and then again,
who would even remember her name
this young woman
if she followed?
she hears a voice from indoors
from behind the shutters
a mother's voice.
'Dorothea! you forgot your shawl!'
the young woman turns.
'Come in, my love!'
the pavement looks away
 'Come in from the night....'
'And bring the cat in!'

9. WORD

Today
suddenly butterflies
the first of summer
words spring to mind
petalootha
schmeterling
metelyk
baboshka
farfalla
each spoken version
for the silence of them.

BERLIN
(2016/22)

AFTER XMAS

Three days gone
one day till your return
I have already forgotten your face…
It is a trick
not to be believed
a heart's trick
of the mind and its divisions
that wants
and doesn't want
from too much wanting,
a gift
stowed and blindfold
hidden from myself
and its childish grasping,
so much the better
for the waiting
for the openings of doors and coats
and that moment
that will unwrap
your face and form
in the doorway,
and neither you nor I

of one piece in ourselves
nor ever will be,
yet mind and parts regardless
the sum of our difference
will make the whole.

for Emily, Hasenheide.

ALLERHEILIGEN, HASSENHEIDE CEMETERY

Their names
Martha
Karl
Familienname : Leise
together, their neglected grave
its ivy and overgrowth
where we lit a candle to these strangers
to forgotenness
to the darkening afternoon
to our colours
my pale blue suit and scarf
you in your green skirt
bright as neon you insisted
the grey
the turquoise
legs red
in red stockings
And the others
our list of lovers past
a dare and an inventory

and devised each others funeral speeches
and who would be the first
with winter at our heels
and each of us
our coughs
in the weight of this playground
to the monumental dead
and home
to the lightness of things
an egg
for the cat
a half-forbidden cigarette
the key in the door.
Laughter is blind
to past and future
and the weight of solid things
simply slipped our minds.

A SOCIALIST CHRISTMAS 1916/2016.

The wounds no longer deep
and love
once had its reasons

Out of the trenches
crossing the divide
of no-man's land
we played
replayed together
not that game with the ball
but the game of memory
game of forgiveness
game of love
the shouts and screams
the rules that simply made it up
as it went along.

Then back to our separate positions
Nightfall
Rain on the tin roofs
We slept in our overcoats
and wrote of it :
a letter home.

SOCK

Mother
darn this sock
the red one
you know the one I mean
This night
this bedside
you seated next to me
once more
to share this dark
this work
ten years parted
our difference this
mine the privilege
of living dreams,
that still,
that at least.
Life. Some things need repair
the red one
the wear on it
the tear
you know the one I mean
Mother
darn this sock.

NEW YEAR/SYLVESTER

After the bells
after the fireworks
and the shouts
and flirts
and old friends
and new friends
after one too many
too much of time
too much of anything
the old year
left his hat and scarf
on the trolleybus seat
fell down a stairwell
made a fool of himself
just for the hell
of it
slipped
on something unpleasant
had words with
somebody's dog
considered his shadow
under a streetlight

lost his wallet
couldn't care less
tripped
over
a brick
lost his overcoat
lost a shoe
lost his way home
nothing but wreckage
doesn't give a damn
and sleeps
on the railway track.

VOLKSPARK

each season its contagion
each its story
love
and then a walk perhaps
along a sunlit shore
then that season of melancholy
then perhaps a common cold
and how we failed the lesson
of the seen it before
of curtains
and openings
and closings
the swelling narrative
and how our storyteller lost its nerve
and quit the premises
and took its name off the programme notes
and skulks away
and leaves us to our seats and stalls
and the bitter guilt and shame
of cheap endings
and up from our benches
and down the aisle of winter

this winter's Volkspark
in our heavy shoes and overcoats
how we could only see it coming
how he will strip her of her green millions
and bask and freeze
content in the repose
of his impeccable coolness
comes as nobody's surprise
the plot
is lost
fuck it
where's the bar?
Intermezzo.

SUNFLOWER FIELD
IN AUTUMN

Then we rose in air
the earth beneath us
ten thousand strong
and destiny
around our gilded heads
we were admirable
high as a gunshot
the scented stars
turned on our faces
and sun and moon
our servants
ushered on before us
down the long march of Summer.

Witness us
fallen now
ragged in glory
necks bowed
blackened
Such is the victory

that sends us out from here
In our death is no defeat
We are set aside
just to return
in earthly light
in russet fire
into the pyre
of Autumn.

BEAST

Beauty sleeps
the beast beside,
love's magic glove nearby
put and folded
next to something
that resembles a marriage bed.
He slips away
one hundred leagues
over the paw-hurting frost
of an unknowable world,
the rush of night and forest
the hunt
the prey
the child
in its first remembered winter
friendless
in the scent of medical waiting rooms
and its tranquilised blood
fear in its mittens
will eye the darkness of some approaching foe
the rush
the crack and break

which is only the future
of what he will become
and night by night
will prey upon himself
himself devour.
Beauty sleeps
the beast beside,
wakes,
in scant recollection,
into another dream,
and lies alongside her.

Athens
(2019/24)

OF BLACK

An August's heat and light
this afternoon
the shade.
Down in the courtyard
the anarchists
are playing ping-pong.
Black is a question mark
of dress-ups
black like night
and all its other similes
black is a statement
of how come
you got so pale
in this tourist season
of trademark sunglasses
and weather forecasts and suncreams?
I joke
the black
has someone died
you answer yes
the death of hope
but that was long ago.

We will wander side by side
in the symmetry
of a trance
we will sleepwalk
our days will be made of dreams
down past the squares and bus stops
up to some apartment door
the light and its blind surfaces
the visible world
unlocks the gate
the watchman
standing watch
how we will speak in
half-agreement
the incontestable manifestos
the swaddling cloth
the winding sheet
and the choice of how and when
how it might go like
some kind of suicide pact perhaps
you and I
perhaps but maybe not today
is not the perfect moment
or all the somethings in between
that's just another thing
there's something missing
there's always something missing
i don't mean you and me
in particular
i mean speaking generally

as we will speak
for now
conditional promises
that could go something like
how we will leave our shadows
this evening
at the doorstep
and step inside
but this in mind:
we can be sure
come morning
I mean the shadows
come morning
they will still be waiting for us

Notara, Athens

CLATTY

Of poverty
lesson of empty pockets
of empty pockets
lesson
of hands
of nowhere in particular
to go
lesson
of shoes
or night and its doorways
lesson of thefts and charities
of strangers
of faces
and other broken things
lesson of sleep
for instance
the ancient dog beside
the nose
the slipway forward
(though memory is a treacherous guide)
a wall to sleep against
beneath the hearts and slogans

of neglected causes
(we are tested)
'After Midnight'
says the shopfront
the wreckers yard
the gravel path
of epitaphs and altars
of upturned eyes upturned in marble faith
of some day soon
when even the famished earth will say
enough
it has had its fill
(and find us wanting)
the fates
(or so they name themselves)
the hardmen
and the knives
and the shopkeepers wives
tonight all doing night-shift
the pavement and its charities
unwanted things all given freely
is not so much to sing about
but sing he shall
and hear him out
and watch him go
his sanctity his just reward
the naked rat under its slab
the black penny
for the pocket
of the clatty man.

RUIN

This dream I had
the pavement cats
stray in and out of it
as they would
any other ruin
and room by derelict room
make a home of it

I will not wake from this
this dream
this place
these cats
we will make a
home together here
our spirits will interbreed
we will multiply
I will multiply

we will walk the town
day into night
one thousand eyes
and footsteps

our furs and types
cat's masks and masquerades
on our faces
pitiable
insolent
down
and out
thieves
and gamblers and chancers
and royalty
kings and queens
as the mood takes us.

we know the ways of men
(our memories are longer, clearer)
how some give pause
and gaze into our upturned
faces
imagining some clue
some half-guessed kinship there
or some forgotten fellowship
and put it down to fancy
and turn away
and go about their business
of men and their ways
the tearing down
the building up
the tearing down again
it will come
the fire and sledgehammer
always has and will

is their concern
no fault of theirs
only their birthright
they bring it on themselves
born as such
into their weakness
their gods have fled them
the abandoned
to the toil and industry
of reap and sow
and gild their nakedness
as best they might
we have no need of such things
neither belonging nor belongings
the kerbs and neighbourhoods
are our chef and architect
and we
we will shoulder our thoughts
and moving on
so move on.

Casa Lapathiotis, Kontouriotou, Exarchia Athens.

BIRTHDAY PARTY

This your other
birthday party
and its gifts
from a Southern city
a paper tablecloth
an empty chair
an empty restaurant
this soup bowl
untouched as yet
the bread as yet unbroken
a beaker of Russian wine
cheap, red, (€1.00)
as over the way
the years strung out in sunlight
on someone's washing line
the years
your years
each in its colour
each in its meaning
hung like flags
and even the strays are out
(I have never seen so many)
out from the haunted rubble and

abandoned doorways
and look at me inquiringly this evening
out of their cat's faces
but they do not talk of hunger
not this evening
nor of ghosts
nor of shyness
but sing of you
song of the cats
αδεσποτα
of the nameless
that you may never
learn the lesson of invisibility
nor tread cautiously
nor timidly
nor ever shrink
from hands put forth in gentleness
but roam the nights and alleyways
home of silent
and imaginary things
that you may never fail
the art of leap
and balance
that you may never
stray:
and sing of you
one thousand voices strong
this evening
from this city Athens,
this paper tablecloth
this Southern city.

For Emily.

BAR

every bar
should have a cat
a small black cat
like this one
for the big guys
the hardmen
in their black tee-shirts
and cards and hard drink
hard talk
and the
invincible protocols
of tough
and its variations
For every bar
a small street cat like this one
message
messenger
from quite another world
to every bar
a cat
and hard hands
under tabletops

shyly dispatched
and tenderness requested
and granted in return
brings comfort
on the sneak
comforts the heart.

Raccoon Bar, Neapolis Athens

LATERNA

Blizzard
and the school choir cancelled
snow on rooftops
and a silent companion
a dog that fell
through the ice
of this remembered afternoon
remembered winter
the moon
is a cold lover
a coin
under the pillow
of this day's sleep
our evening's footsteps
the kafenion
the evening balconies
the climbing teams
climb skywards
as we shuffle in below
my love
do not look down
the drop

is not worth the fall
as in some ancient song
the street
the ancient grinder
Thessaloniki
and his barrel organ
follows on behind.

HAT

What gave with the rain
that afternoon
how come it didn't happen
then came of a sudden
down from Lycavitos
like a sea
over the street?
and I watched it from some wreck
of a sheltering doorway
and thought I saw
borne past on the flood
the hat
the trilby hat
a gift
a Berlin theatre friend
who lavished attention for a time
then grew tired of me
then competitive
then grew to despise me :
time is a parenthesis
between two oblivions
two floods

at least we
once agreed on that
lost friend
and so the storm
and so the hat
the street
and its vanishing point
into the tides of bitter recollection
and forgetting
the sluice
of what the hat brought
of what the flood brought
and washed
and bore away.

MOLOTOV

Let fly the Molotovs!
greetings
from planet utopia!
Planet state replies
the gift of gas canisters!
we bring you tears
for your paradise!
They are shouting again
I do not know why
I only know they frighten me
and someone hurt
at the end of it.

Forgive me
I am just a passer-by
in these matters
and always have been
nor a woman from around these parts
nor from anywhere in particular
if you cared to ask.

It seems to me

What futures
lie hidden
clenched inside these
upraised fists
is anybody's business

It seems to me
the price of bread
is the mother of it all
and that is the leaven of it.

the choice is tasked
one slogan or another
it all comes to the same
and I my common mind
my common understanding
that man may
find a home
in itself
that is all I ask
and want to ask
and there the end of it.

FACE

You are without a face.
I will draw your eyes.
I will draw your lips.
If I do not draw your feet,
you will not walk away from me.
I will do what I can.
I cannot draw your mind.
I cannot draw your voice.
I will draw my heart
in rough resemblance to yours,
and how your hand describes me
white like chalk
against a night like slate.
More, is yours alone.
You will draw my feet so I may step closer
next to you,
and your heart
in fair resemblance to mine,
in hope and its approximations,
this sketch,
this line.

With Tea Hodzic, Athens/Sarajevo

ESTHER

Heat: F 1600
Time: 1hr per 50 Kgs
Hell's kitchen
one imagines
a furnace
in a municipal three-piece suit
and the boys
end of line
with their gloves and facemasks
and trowels and ashes
and the box
the cardboard box.
Which is not the point.
The point is you
Esther Pantazis.
First
that last breakfast in Arizona
you were trouble then
that was commonly said
and the breakfast vodka
(count me in)
and sang the fiercest Gershwin

and that women's song from childhood Mykonos
a song you knew I loved
something like :
'I will go down to the sea if I say so
and my hands an oar
and my chest a sail
and return to shore again.'
And your fingernails dug into my forearm
like I wasn't listening properly.

Next
some Summers passed
high Summer Crete
that's you now Esther
from over the Atlantic
a rattling sound
a cardboard box.
We climbed up to the Dictean cave
the Americans and I
David and Nancy and the others
under an August sun
Up on the summit
dark in there and a sudden chill
and down the long stairwells
to where the lake lay
deep inside the mountain
black as night, untroubled, smooth as glass
deep home and haven
one imagined
for all the eyeless of this world.
And so

a dip into the opened box
the ashes scattered
then brushed off my hands
of the dust and gravel
onto my trouser leg
and saw you
so I think
for the briefest moment
figure in an ashen nightdress
bare of foot
lain out in state
of sorts
on the water's bier
and as suddenly gone.
The waters received you.
Of gifts that can't be given
given anyway
of infinities to come
the blind conjecture
but my wish
each season in its turn
years in their turn
to you
Esther
an endless year
of thirteen moons.

OTHER
(2016/22)

SHOE

Emma almost made it home
after that evening
Emma
how drunk we got
I saw you to the taxi
I'm told you almost
made it to the door
and left instead
a single shoe
out in that night's rain
outside on the pavement.

Patrick
it's morning now
sure
something she said to me
something about an old school friend
a place to live
a coast
a chance
listen
its not the time

not just now
just get off the phone to me
and
hold that shoe to your ear
and maybe
you might just
hear
the sea.

VISIT

He will say
now
it's nothing
it's just the moon in your window
the rest
is just a waste of candlelight
comedy of sorrows
song
of the empty bottles
it's nothing
he will say
and even the trolley bus
spoke your name
a rented room
in sleep
is no escape
nor death
who speaks her distance
in chimes and sleighbells
over the ice and cold
of this night:
he is numb

he is immaterial
the visitor
he is the ghost
at your bedside.

OWL

And we rise in air
the earth beneath us
over the rooftops
over the crossroads
what sound does a cloud make?
over the parasols and bonnets
of your festive midnight
over your lanterns, ribbons
laughter, dancesteps, ball gowns
sound of your accordions
a provenance of mice
we float and fall
swallow you whole
into the grinding tract
the winding gut
and skull and skeleton
sick you out
and cast you from our
towers and treetops :
we are told
we are the creatures of darkness
creatures of the night

yet the divine attendants of Minerva
also Athena
so the handservants of wisdom
the bringers of light.

ORPHEUS

He is naked
bar the ivy on his head
long decades past
since they smelted down the gods
recasting them as angels
and cathedrals
and that instrument of torture
they so worship.
He fled and took refuge
up to his knees
in the sanctuary of this swamp
but the birds come daily to him
bringing nuts and berries
and sun and moon attend him
and when he sings
even the mangroves weep.
Night falls
rekindling the lamp of her absence.
Was that the voice we heard that evening?
out of the dark
of an abolished world
where even her ghost is relegated to mere legend
and a stream of light rushed in on us
a flood of sadness and delight.

APRIL

Love and sorrow
spring out of the selfsame earth
each in its form
each in its moment
one colour at a time.

the songbirds
and their mad songsheets
that obstinate Spring
fully a year past
veiw from your window
garden, vine
in bud
window, sickroom
that bright season's daylight
brightening
the deathbed.

funeral
I ask you
which black should i wear?
the black of which night?
the night we met
the plum brandy

the dawn
the river
summer in its freshness
next
the night we had the good sense
not to become lovers
night
made of couches
supper tables
overcoats on floors
the laughter in the back
of London taxis ;
that black
I think
will suit us very well

and while I'm at it
heaven, paradise, eternity
whatever you call yourself
memory, loss, love
is ours alone
it's not your property
give it back
the rest you can keep.

April : sorrow and love
spring out
of the selfsame earth
each in its moment
each in its form
one colour at a time.

Memoriam. For Gayle.

A SCOTTISH ISLANDER
TO A WEST AFRICAN FRIEND

We were not like you,
not dispossesed
and sold into slavery.
We were dispossesed
and sold into industry.

Up there, the North
an island cottage
rubble and
the empty chimney chain
over a struck-dumb hearth
a story
in some forgotten tongue
sleeps
under a stone
in its bed of rust
A man inside a song
once labored this evening hill
up from the loch
a silver darling

in his apron pocket
a table laid
of hunger
and its iron plate
the blighted root
and its eviction note
to guide their footsteps
down to the ships in waiting
once and all
out of this place
of this tree
a century grown
under a roofless sky
rowan tree
its berries
this early Autumn
red as blood.

This is our story
our part of the bargain
down here
city Glasgow
we caught on fast
we were as we were told we were
we were young animals
we were unteachable
indolence was our uniform
white on red
our fists like flowers
flowered in their playgrounds
our day by day transgression

was our instructor
our weekly wage packet
nightly waste and ruin

our stories
you and I
dare brook few comparisons
only the journey out
and back
perhaps these broken links
the twists and forks
of the uncaptive mind
city Glasgow
we were wild animals
we were unteachable
yet to this advantage
we taught ourselves
our minds
are our own
to this benefit:
our minds
are our revenge.

Cameroon / Isle of Skye

OLD MOON

The old moon is dead.
Listen carefully
the dogs are laughing at the dark
of the uncertain hope
of rebirth
uncertain knowledge
of a sickle light to come.

Shelter me
old moon
put me under your overcoat
the shabbiness, the smell
it's nothing
How does the moon smell?
We will wander side by side
you and I
we will drift this obscurity
two tramps
no need to go begging the light
the light will come.

You will rise
I will borrow your parachute
down through the days and nights
until my feet tell me
it is done.

Moon
you well know our type
always true to our word
(of course)
constantly going on about you
through the generations
I will return this borrowed thing
of silk, light, clouds
you name it
I will get it back to you
I promise
at my earliest convenience
in the form
of a poem.

STREET OF MARIGOLDS
(INDIA)

Nation of marigolds
gold of marigolds
marigold thanksgivings
pavement
dressed in marigold
of soles of unshod feet
shod gold
in marigolds
this evening of celebration
a bedside story
told in marigold
of sunsets
parasols
trinkets
buffaloes
marigold elephants
of marigold confectioneries
marigold philosophies

by wicker candlelight
bowl on study windowsill

book unopened
down in the lane
this evening
the rickshaw boys
are singing *Bajan*
to the drum
of broken water pots
and metal hubcaps
it will go on all night
this month of springtime
night of *Holi*
the gods
their garlanded heads
are satisfied
smiling
pleased with us:
a cast-off sandal
on the petalled stairwell
a painted hand
the scattered rice
a strewn kiss
a careless benediction
this night of benedictions
of footsteps
of the figure of the
half-unexpected visitor
of his sandals
in the doorway

I will set down the pewter jug
the bread unbroken

cup and bowl
the household plate and spoon
for the silent companion
the solitary candle flame
its scented shadows
over face and hands
the water
cooled by evening
an earthen jar
such things befitting
such a guest
who will not decline me
nor countenance apology
for the poverty of what I am

Guest leads me by the elbow
to the upper window
guest looks quietly downwards
that I should follow his gaze :
street of prayer
this evening
street of petals
street
of marigolds.

Down in the lane
the rickshaw boys
are singing
(it will go on all night).

Santiniketan/Athens

TALK

Winter comes
any hour now
everything is put away
when I have slept and eaten
when I am no longer drunk
I will write to you
I admit
I cannot recollect your shoes
these recent days
neither style nor colour
enough to say
the days have left you barefoot
only that blue shirt
you were so proud of
blue
the blue of cornflowers

They say you have been ill
they say your appearance
is much changed
so people talk
as they once spoke of us

or god knows even now
how they may still
speak

they say you no longer mention me
they say you sometimes do
so people talk
come off it men
face it
we have that much in common
so she came to Europe
everyone fell in love with her
our difference being
I made no secret of it
you and I
let loose
let side by side
into that place
that called itself Italy
out onto the fields and lanes
driven mad
out of the wreck
of an illogical summer

there is no gossip
worth the mention
without another's pain
at heart of it
so people talk
they will say you were reckless
for want of anything better

to speak of
of well-kept secrets
unseen story
like that August summer's
iron heat
how we dived
that one last time
like every afternoon
for the cool of it
beneath the surface of the lake
but only this last time
failed to reappear

I would speak
of the stubborn nature
of memory
and its inhabitants
the scent revisited
of orange peel
and crushed geraniums
scent of
a ruined bed
and you still waiting
seated on the farmhouse steps there
much as before
brushing the night from your hair
as memory would have it
like nothing has really happened
like scarcely a day had passed

this issue of self-knowing
sits badly with me
memory endures
memory risks
the simple argument
of its own experience
no gain the talk
and prophecies of regret
nor profit in remembered harms
the poverty of watchfulness
in this cold season
rather
the touch
of a rug
the priviledge of nakedness
the upended heart
and laughter
at the embarrassment of being
rather to hear
what once we heard
in the wager of listening
hear what we hear
in silence and its risk
and the hazard we speak
when we speak of love.

CATALOGUE
DES POUBELLES # 6.

I caught your eye
in morning's light
a hall of mirrors
shone within you
disordered geometries
your dress-up
light and shade
of intersected planes
tangents
parabolics
your palette
crimsons and viridians
outshone the natural world
a chainstore carry bag
your raincloud
a tilted box
a mountaintop
and I stood
and godless thoughts occurred to me
that we are all so much landfill
is our eternity and paradise to come
and it occurs to me
what will Cezanne make of you?

CATALOGUE
DES POUBELLES # 5.

I watched your torment
they grappled you
the cruelty and noise and agony
the mechanized dustcart
and scourged and dumped you here
abandoned like for dead
on this roadside
and left you here for empty
but they will never empty you
nor you go hungry
there is no such thing as emptiness
what was filled
will fill again
evening gathers
in your iron gut
like darkness in a darkened pool
where virgin night emerges
freshly bathed
and I
the first

to cross the street
step up to her
the smallest privilege
a candle lit
this crushed and empty
cigarette pack
this polystyrene coffee cup
cold
as yet unfinished
this thought
this offering
of unfinished things
unfinished thoughts.

CATALOGUE
DES POUBELLES # 2.

Who cares?
call us what we are
sons and daughters
the orphans
of your disordered gluttony
you are the very bowels
that birthed us here
the hand that sweeps us away
only to return again
and hang your street corners
the insolence on our faces
we are
the unforgiving
underhanded comment
as you hurry by
the very soul and voice of
misrule and disorder
and no mistaking it
we are the inconvenient truth
the enemy beneath your feet

we can only multiply
our voices will not go unheard:
if things go on like this
believe us
no less than you deserve
you guys
it can only get worse
for you.

SCHERZO NON TROPPO PRESTO (1)

The planets, moon sun and stars
all in the back of a black taxi cab
laughter
in the heavens.
Driver,
don't take offense
we're just simple tourists
but who'd have thought this ride
through the infinite
could be such fun?
Driver,
let's go round again!

Vine Leaves Press

Enjoyed this book?
Go to *vineleavespress.com* to find more.
Subscribe to our newsletter:

www.ingramcontent.com/pod-product-compliance
Ingram Content Group UK Ltd.
Pitfield, Milton Keynes, MK11 3LW, UK
UKHW040306170625
6427UKWH00002B/38